2:22

a poetic memoir by jada davis

illustrations by emily tigges

trigger warning:

this poetry collection contains themes of: suicide, drug abuse
and sexual assault

dedicated to...

those who are hurt, heartbroken, & healing.

table of contents:

3/25/22 5:55 pm

i'm writing to ensure you'll weep

as you read back this verse

i know you can't help but miss me

my final words for you

shall sting and rehash

even the deepest of wounds

him

12/01/21 1:11 pm

i can't take your pain away
but let me brighten up your day
last night's confessions were full of regret
make it up to me on the hill next sunset?
we envision our future, reminisce the past
admitting nothing's forever, but praying this will last
opening my eyes without a trace of thought
admiring our canvas, dipped in navy and apricot

12/10/21 6:02 pm

as i fall asleep, he comes around every now and then
no longer by coincidence that we meet once again
before him, i was so afraid of the dark
not being able to see what's directly in front of me
until his eyes shined my way and lit up the spark
how come only in the dusk is when he fills up my heart?

i dread as the sun rises
for his love fades away
awakened to a quiet phone and an empty soul
only in my dreams is where he'll stay

i once heard that
your fantasies become reality
when you push fear aside
there's nothing you can't achieve
so if all i want is you
what is there left to do
then fall into a slumber
rather than staying awake to wonder,
"why won't you make the first move?"

12/13/21 4:04 pm

you're clearly the main character
and i'm a bit nervous for auditions
it's been a long time
since i've shined bright on someone's stage
waiting to see which role i get cast as
dreaming of portraying the quirky sidekick
but i'll probably get placed in the ensemble
swaying in the background, humming your song
either way, grateful i even got a part

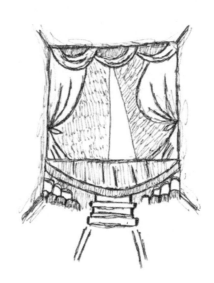

12/18/21 3:07 pm

my hand caressing your cheek
my head buried in your neck
your head spinning in circles
your hand intertwined in mine
soft moans and sweet nothings
feeling empty when you leave
feeling everything when you're near
knowing you're an angel
guarding my heart
even if it isn't yours

12/19/21 3:35 pm

maybe it wasn't quite like the movies
no fireworks exploding in the night sky
our names far from written in the stars
feelings spaced 6 feet apart

but still, i prefer that over
those butterflies that land in my stomach
fluttering up my lungs
taking my breath away

fearing those monarchs will morph into monsters
eating me alive from the inside out
my anxiety turning to anguish
my passion persisting into pain...

...yet this emptiness is surreal
i'm savoring the solace in your safety

us

12/21/21 6:05 pm

entanglement
tangled in a web of what if's
tiptoeing the fine line
between what is "right" and "wrong"
my sweet trapeze artist
spinning circles inside my mind
my heart pirouettes
every time your name
is even uttered
my knees grow weak
and i sigh in defeat
when i realize
i'm not the only girl
you've put on this show for

12/23/21 11:48 pm

i start every sunrise by beginning to brew
some discounted decaf
an attempt to avoid fixating on you

remember when i had you with sugar and cream?
well, things aren't like they used to be
i now stir in a splash of scotch
it's the easiest way to kick life up a notch
after all, numbing my body and brain
is much easier than dealing with this pain

i no longer need you to get me through my day
i'd rather burn my throat and dilute my worries away
so i won't choke up when they ask if i'm okay

12/25/21 3:00 am

the spotlight shines on the least graceful ballerina
knocking one too many glasses over
spilling toxicity onto the hardwood floor
soaking up sorrow with a stained sweat rag
making a mess inside his safe haven
the only place he rehearses his routine
he pliés until his legs give out
and can only sleep with his feet
tucked into first position
we tiptoe over sharp shards
every single time we have a conversation
yet, after i shut the door
i have to open up my junk drawer
to search for bandaids
that'll cover my bruises

12/26/21 1:38 am

this is now
the sixth time
we've said our final goodbyes
swearing to the sky
we'll stop tiptoeing this fine line
until temptation creeps in
and once again
your lips meet mine

12/27/21 10:02 pm

post nut clarity

isn't usually this bittersweet

when your white tank top

is draped over my body

like a tattered wedding gown

but we are so far from the cathedral

i have said i do

time after time

while you, yet again

left me stranded at the altar

12/28/21 10:24 am

if you truly tried
to "be that guy" for me
please explain why
so many conversations
begin and end
the moment i start to cry?

i sound childish, i'm well aware
but i know a man who loves me
wouldn't dare leave me to believe
that my emotions are too much to bare

12/30/21 2:01 am

i know when he falls asleep
and envisions his future wife and family
i'm nowhere near the girl of his dreams
truthfully, nobody actually desires me

a list of shortcomings, where do i begin?
i'd rather pray for love than repent my own sins
my so-called "beauty" only shines from within
because his mom despises the color of my skin
yet, despite my attempts to change myself for him
love is a losing game that I was never meant to win

12/31/21 3:33 am

i don't know when your phone alarm will ring
with its label reading:
"there's someone better"
but we both know
you'll never find anyone quite like me
every last smile your eyes lay upon
will be compared to mine
one day you'll wake up in a cold sweat
trembling when you turn and find
my face isn't next to yours
you're left insecure and wondering
what could've been
knowing i'm the one that got away
praying i fall for someone new
when you're the one who pushed me off the cliff

her

1/2/22 10:33 pm

who knew that when the ball dropped
my heart would come along for the ride
when i shattered onto his pavement
and no one could clean up my pieces

how does a party so quickly turn into a funeral
mourning the loss of what once was
i didn't think i was dressed for the occasion
until i realized i was already wearing all black
and the guests kept offering me tissues

1/07/22 5:23 pm

lucky for you
i forgot what it's like to pop pills
to numb my pain through restless nights
and wash them down with an unholy spirit

she's since started serving them to me
two perfectly sliced halves
on a silver platter
not knowing
that before i close my eyes
i curse her name under my breath
because even though she needs me
it's as if i have to attend
a party i was never asked to be invited to
but i look like the asshole
if i dare disappoint our guests

1/09/22 7:06 pm

i laid lonesome, tucked in a makeshift casket
i hadn't left that room for 18 hours
till i craved a single piece of candy
a subtle hint of sweetness for the road ahead
i navigated toward the staircase
engine running on empty
till i was greeted to a pair of doe eyes
a single tear rushed down my face

"would you even miss me?"
crouched on the bottom step
my jagged fingernails dragged against his soft fur
"because, i think i'll miss you most of all."
his paws scurried away
without a care in the world
i've come to terms with my eviction
a note and keys upon a spotless nightstand

1/08/22 5:23pm

"i know... but it's too soon."
that's what he told me, at least
his sweet brown eyes
gazed deep into mine
as he leaned into whisper
"it's not your time"

i wrapped my arms around him
when i squeezed harder
she turned to me
asked why i'm hugging the air
there's no easy way of telling her
that i ran into the man
who left far too soon
and begged him to drive me away...

...he said he was sorry
but i'd have to find another way home

2/06/22 1:14 am

"how come you haven't dated a girl yet?"
truthfully, men have always been a safer bet
even if every heartbreak coincides with regret
why take time to work through my trauma
when instead, a new boy could help me forget?

meanwhile, she barely gives me attention
her eyes wouldn't dare look in my direction
until it's time to cry over some dumbass guy
there's no way someone so beautiful
would give somebody this damaged a try

1/25/22 7:36 pm

i woke up to a lifeless body

covered in bruises, half of which

i don't quite remember the source of

did he leave behind a single love bite

or a failed attempt to mark his territory?

either way,

i am nothing but damaged goods

just offer me a single compliment

the slightest hint of validation

and next thing you know

we'll be linked arm in arm

stumbling out of this parking deck together

2/01/22 1:12 pm

in attempts to move on from you

i tried to bottle up my baggage

instead, i silently sobbed against our driveway

gasping for air, grasping the foreclosure sign

for i can no longer find shelter in your arms

2/10/22 9:18 pm

i despise you for tricking me to believe

we were once two lonely fishes

that swam together deep in the sea

until the day you left me astray

after i had wish and washed

your every last worry away

2/14/22 5:59 pm

i can't even process my pain

let alone type tales of trauma

into carefully constructed sentences

i'm no longer able to seek refuge

shielded behind pillars of prose

that would suffice for our silent suffering

i'll never forgive you for abandoning me

in the aftermath of a vicious storm

that stripped away my every last word

epilogue

4/06/22 2:22 am

if i never learned how to swim
why ponder over waves i'd miss?
after drowning deep into an ocean
whose current sucked me in its abyss

for so long, i felt destined to soar and fly
amidst vast stars or across twilight skies
yet, i can't explain why i start to cry
when a strike of lightning merely passes by

whether my sinful soul is meant
to rise high and reach the divine
or sink below amongst the unknown
i believe when i surrender myself
onto my knees, kissing the ground beneath
God will grant me the strength to survive

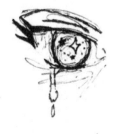 

about the author:

jada davis is an award winning writer and podcaster. born and raised in central new jersey, she excelled in writing throughout her early years, placing in her township's slam poetry competition at age 14. davis went on to receive multiple national awards for her journalistic articles and self-produced podcasts. she has since earned an associates  degree in communications, achieving highest honors. she currently attends rutgers university, pursuing her bachelor's degree in public relations. alongside her poetic endeavors, davis has been co-hosting and managing 5wpodcast since 2019. 2:22 is davis' first poetry book, and certainly won't be her last.

follow her on instagram: @jldpoems

about the illustrator:

through creativity, emily tigges has become an accompanied artist. at age 16, tigges' artwork was published in her first book. alongside this, her artwork was presented in a township art show located in new jersey. tigges used her brilliant creativity to open her own small business selling her diverse creative arts.

follow her on instagram: @emilyymaliaa

Printed in Great Britain
by Amazon

23483171R00020